D1550476

"For educators who want to develop their practice and 'break the mould' of our more traditional teaching practices this book would be a great starting point."

Peter Kirby, Life Education Centres

"… an extraordinary book. It is the cleverest, simplest, funniest and most engaging treatise on thinking skills available."

Paul Ginnis, author of *The Teacher's Toolkit*

"… a must for every home and every classroom. Ian Gilbert brings us hope that not only educationalists but also parents will want to share and develop the way we think about thinking. It is also a delightful story in its own right with very loveable characters."

Ron Gandolfo, Headteacher, Lingfield Primary School

"… another gem from the pen of Ian Gilbert! From the opening lines the reader is taken on an exploration—of how, what, why and where we think and learn but also an exploration of oneself, one's relationship with people, places and the mysteries of the natural and created world."

Kathy Alcock, Principal Lecturer in Education, Canterbury Christ Church University College

"… amusing, witty, thought provoking and an original way of introducing thinking skills"

Dr David George, Educational Consultant, Gifted Education

"Many recent books have begun to acknowledge the great importance of thinking skills in education, but Ian Gilbert takes this theme further by actively exploring how these thinking skills can relate to the development and potential of both the individual and society. Making this profound area accessible to young people, in particular, is no easy task, but Little Owl achieves it admirably. Whether you are a teacher, parent, pupil, or just plain curious, *Little Owl's Book of Thinking* will provide some invaluable food for thought, learning and life."

Will Ord, Chair of SAPERE (Society for the Advancement of Philosophical Enquiry and Reflection in Education)

Little Owl's Book
of Thinking

Ian Gilbert

Crown House Publishing
www.crownhouse.co.uk

First published by

Crown House Publishing Ltd
Crown Buildings, Bancyfelin, Carmarthen, Wales, SA33 5ND, UK
www.crownhouse.co.uk

and

Crown House Publishing Ltd
P.O. Box 2223, Williston, VT 05495-2223, USA
www.CHPUS.com

© Ian Gilbert 2004
Illustrations © Virginia Mayo

The right of Ian Gilbert to be identified as the author of this work has
been asserted by him in accordance with the Copyright, Designs and
Patents Act 1988.

All rights reserved. Except as permitted under current
legislation no part of this work may be photocopied, stored in a retrieval
system, published, performed in public, adapted, broadcast, transmitted,
recorded or reproduced in any form or by any means,
without the prior permission of the copyright owners.
Enquiries should be addressed to
Crown House Publishing Limited.

British Library Cataloguing-in-Publication Data
A catalogue entry for this book is available
from the British Library.

ISBN 190442435X

LCCN 2004106208

Printed and bound in the UK by
The Cromwell Press
Trowbridge
Wiltshire

To William
If only he would read it

Contents

Why?

It's amazing what you can do on a train bound for Exeter. (I wasn't bound for Exeter, the train was. I was going to Reading. Which is ironic given that I wrote a book. A bit like going to Barking to buy a dog. Or Brent for a goose.)

What came out on my journey were the bare bones of the book you are about to read—years of research, teaching and experience about how young people can use their brains more effectively squeezed into seven chapters, two owls, a whole forest of woodland creatures but no very small sheep.

What was in the back of my mind—wherever that is—was the thought of a father reading the book to his child and getting as much from it as his son or daughter. Maybe even more.

There are many good books on the shelves about thinking and learning. Some of them are very good. Indeed some of them are so good they have been written many, many times.

But given the fact that I am trying to encourage a more creative way of thinking in my readers the only way this book could be written is in a way that no-one else has.

As a very wise Roman owl called Horace once said with some irony, "Bis repetita placent".[*]

Or as we say where I'm from: "Do things no-one does or do things everyone does in a way no-one does."

Like a stereo in a lift, this book works on many different levels. There's no need to worry if not

---

[*] Literally translated 'the more you like it, the more you'll get it'. And then we're only one small step away from focus groups.

everyone gets them all. (Although be slightly worried if no-one gets any.) Above all the book is designed to make you laugh and make you think. But not necessarily always in that order.

Any one of the areas covered can be built on in a conversation with your child or your class. Ask them how they feel about taking responsibility or breaking the rules. What does it mean to them to have such a powerful brain? What do they think about when they think about thinking?

See if they can identify if their preferred way of learning is through their eyes, through their ears or just getting to grips with what it is to be learned.

And what about their different intelligence strengths? For those of you new to education (or who have been in education for a very, very long time) multiple intelligences theory was developed by a wise American owl called Howard. He suggests that we all have strengths and weaknesses across at least eight different sorts of intelligence. Which means there's so much more to intelligence than the you'reeither-clever-or-you're-not IQ approach to things.

Which means that you can ask your child not how smart they are but how are they smart?

Then see what happens.

So, sit back, snuggle up or do whatever it is that you need to do to prepare for a woodland walk that may change the way you think about thinking.

And remember to be careful where a simple train journey may take you. Especially if you are heading north to Ramsbottom.

Firstly

"How do you do it, Dad?" asked Benny, the owlet.

(For those of you who don't know, an owlet is a little owl, as piglet is a little pig, and outlet is a little out but not all the way.)

"Do what?" said Big Owl, Benny the Owlet's dad, who being grown up didn't need letters after his name.

"Be so wise and all knowing?"

"Well," replied the wise middle-aged owl, "I think it's just an owl thing. To be honest I am not really sure how I got to be omniscient."

"Will I be wise like you when I'm all grown up?" asked Benny, who was too small to appreciate semantic irony.

"Well," said Big Owl, "that depends on how you think."

"Think about what?" asked Benny.

"No. Just think," came the reply.

Benny looked confused and frustrated in a head-swivelling-blink-one-eye-at-a-time-slowly-owly sort of way.

"Nope, you've lost me there," he replied. "I mean I *do* think, all the time, don't I? Don't I? You can't *not* think. It's just natural. Like growing feathers and swooping on mice so silently that they don't even know they're dead until you cough up the crunchy bits."

"You might well be born thinking," replied Big Owl, "but that doesn't mean to say you can't do it better. It's like driving a car. Everyone can learn, so everyone can learn to do it even better."

"How do you know about driving a car? You're just an owl," asked Benny, keen to catch out his dad, like the time when he claimed to have invented the Toilet Owl only to have had his idea stolen by the ducks.

"I'm your dad *and* I'm an owl—that doesn't leave much scope for ignorance," replied Big Owl huffily, easy for a wolf, harder for an owl. "And another thing," he continued, resuming where he had left off, which is always a good place to resume anything. "Never say *just* an owl. It's like when you give someone a ring on the telephone—so I'm told," he added quickly before Benny could question the validity of his claim, "and start your conversation with, 'It's *only* me.' If you belittle yourself, why should others think big of you?"

"Fair point," said Benny who in actual fact wasn't going to question the phone thing because he had assumed that, as a bird, his dad knew about ringing. Although what people say, what they mean and what other people hear are so often three different things.

"So, what you're saying," said Benny, trying to keep up, "is that, even though I think, I can think better, and the better I think the more chance there is that I will become old and wise like you."

"Well, the 'old' bit just happens," said Daddy with a resigned look in one of his eyes, "but the 'wise' bit, yes, we can work on that."

"Great," said Benny, "let's start now. If we do it quickly enough I can buck the system and become the world's first wise *young* owl."

Wishing he had thought of that, Big Owl fluffed his feathers in that birdy way you get when you twizzle a mop round really fast. Then he shifted from leg to leg on his perch, easy for an owl to do but time-consuming for a millipede.

"The time is right, I suppose," he said with great solemnity, more to himself than to his son. "Now is the time."

"Time for what?" asked Benny.

"Time to think."

"Think about what?"

"Time to think," said Big Owl seriously, "about thinking."

Benny looked closely at his father's face to see if he was being as serious as he was acting. It didn't take many seconds to realise that indeed he was. Thinking was obviously a serious business.

"You see the oak trees that surround and protect the birds and animals of the forest, providing us all with a home and shelter and somewhere to scratch?" began Big Owl. "We will choose seven of these mighty trees and each one will represent one of the seven thinking principles. This is how I was taught by my father on this very branch of the Home Tree many years ago and this is how he was taught by his father and so on back to the dawn of time when this wood was just … a little wood."

"A woodlet?" suggested Benny.

"No, more of a twiglet," responded Big Owl. "Now, we will take each one in turn and if you have any questions …"

"Yes?" said Benny.

"Then good, because questions mean that we're making progress."

Benny was just about to agree with this last comment, and then realised that it might be a trick, so immediately felt he had to come up with a good question at this point.

"So … er … questions are a good thing, are they, then, Dad?" he asked proudly.

"An unexamined life is a life not worth living," replied Big Owl mysteriously. "And that's a quotation from a wise Mediterranean owl who lived thousands of years ago, so it must be true, no questions asked."

Oak: The First

"The first oak we shall look at is the broadest one in the forest," began Big Owl.

Benny looked around to see which one he meant.

"Which one do you mean?" asked Benny.

"The one in the clearing over there that stands head and shoulders above the rest," replied Big Owl. "This oak represents the awesome power of the thinking brain—your brain. Let me show you. How many branches does it have, Benny?"

Benny looked but didn't know where to start counting (apart from the obvious starting point, which was "one", although he felt that that might be missing the point).

"Lots, Dad," said Benny in awe.

"Big lots," said Big Owl. "And if there are lots of branches how many twigs are there on those lots of branches and how many leaves are there on those lots of twigs?"

"Lots of lots," replied Benny, who had never really thought about trees in this light before.

"Well," said Big Owl, "let's imagine that this tree is your brain, my brain, everyone's brain. Millions and trillions of branches, growing out to connect and crisscross with other branches. Think of each leaf as a brain cell—the building blocks that make up your brain, and each branch and twig as the connections that link all your millions of brain cells together."

Benny screwed his face up a little to see if that would help him with his imagining. Surprisingly, it did.

"Every time you think, you send energy crackling around your brain along connections and between brain cells at up to a hundred and seventy miles per hour. Thousands of branches and twigs and leaves light up in huge shimmering patterns of energy coursing across and around your brain every time you think the simplest of thoughts like, 'What's for lunch?' or, 'What's the capital of Nicaragua?' or, 'How do teapots work?'"

Benny was slowly beginning to grasp what his dad was getting at, although he was a little lost on the teapot bit. He asked his dad to carry on all the same.

"Carry on all the same, Dad," said Benny.

Instead, Big Owl carried on nonetheless, which is like all the same but cleverer.

"The really clever thing is that every time you learn new things you actually grow new branches to make more connections. And, the more connections you have, the more connections you can then go on to have. So, the more you use your brain, the more you can use it! The more you learn ..."

"... the more you *can* learn," finished Benny in amazement, interrupting Big Owl's train of thought so that he could hop aboard too. "So, what you're saying is that I can actually grow the power in my brain by using it and the more I use it the more powerful it gets?"

"Exactly," replied Big Owl, glad to have his son aboard and working up a good head of steam now. "So, your power for thinking is linked to the number of connections you have taken the time to grow—the number of branches and twigs on the oak."

"But that's zillions," said Benny incredulously.

"Yes, my son," said Big Owl, pausing triumphantly. "It is. It has been written that we are all capable of 'hundreds of trillions of thinkable thoughts' and that if you counted every possible connection in your brain it would take you over thirty million years and the number you came up with would wrap itself many times around the whole planet."

Millions, billions, trillions and zillions! Benny's head started to swim—fine for a duck but unsettling for an owl.

"So, your point is …?" asked Benny slowly, staring with wonder at the powerful broad oak.

"My point, my son, is that between your two tucked-away ears you have whatever you need to learn and do whatever you need to learn and do." Benny gulped as he used his brain to think about itself. "So, don't tell me there's anything you can't do because it simply isn't true.

Oak: The Second

Benny was sitting on the big branch of the Home Tree with a faraway smile on his face, still reeling from his new understanding about the staggering power he could now feel pulsating between his ears when Big Owl asked him to look down.

"No, it's OK, Dad," said Benny, "I like being happy."

"No, son," replied Big Owl patiently (who *did* get semantic irony), "look towards the forest floor. What do you see?"

Benny looked at the forest floor intently, but despite these intentions could not see what his father was getting at.

"Go on," urged Big Owl. "Tell me what you see."

"Dead leaves, dead moss, dead twigs, dead branches. Wow! A lot of dead things. I get your point, Dad," Benny continued, missing the point altogether, as so often happens when someone claims to get someone else's point. "You live, you have an amazing brain, and then you die and become nothing more than decomposing litter to be eaten by flies and maggots and very small sheep."

"No," replied Big Owl, "that's not what I mean at all. What do you see growing out of all that rubbish?" And then he added with a loving force, "Look carefully, my son, look carefully."

Benny stared down at the forest floor from his perch and began to see—or rather notice, which is a very different thing from see—all manner of things he had never seen, let alone noticed, before.

"Wow!" he said, his beak dropping open. "Look at that!"

He saw the colours of the leaves—more shades of brown than in a nineties fashion show. He noticed tiny universes of lichen and moss of such intricate detail that it took his breath away. He noticed the way that the sunlight dripped through the branches of the trees and lay in pools across the forest floor. And he saw tiny little oak trees, some no more than a twig with one or two leaves to wave, pushing themselves up through the hustle and bustle of the forest floor.

"Tiny oaks!" said Benny. "They must be oaklets."

"Yes," said Big Owl, "they sort of are."

Big Owl continued, "Now look around you at all of the trees in the forest. Each and every one of them started in exactly the same way. No more than a twig with a leaf or two. All right, some may have grown up in nicer areas with more light or more space than others, but they all started out in exactly the same way."

Benny took a deep breath because he could feel his second lesson approaching.

"What will that little oak become, do you think?" asked Big Owl.

"Yes I do," replied Benny answering the last part of the question first, "and as for the oak, I don't know—a big oak?"

"A very big oak—that's exactly right. The most royal tree in the forest. A tree fit for a king to hide out in, and an outlaw, although not at the same time, obviously."

"Or in the same tree."

"Quite. Now, my son, tell me: if the oak becomes a big oak, what might you become?"

"A big owl," replied Benny with what he was sure would be misplaced confidence.

"Yes, that's right," replied Big Owl, much to Benny's surprise. "And, like the oak, you have no choice in the matter, do you? It just sort of happens, doesn't it? Your body knows what to do. But ..."

Benny always knew a "but" meant trouble and much preferred it when his dad said "and".

"But, what about your *mind*?"

"My mind?" asked Benny, getting that all-over confused feeling again. "What about my mind?"

"What does your mind want you to become, Benny?"

To be honest, Benny didn't know. "I honestly don't know," he said without a word of a lie. "I haven't really thought. I mean, it all just happens, doesn't it, like growing up? I mean, do I have to work out what *sort* of owl I want to become?"

"So, you don't really care about what sort of owl you are, what sort of life you have? Is that what you're saying?"

"No," replied Benny with indignation, "I'm not saying that at all. It's just, well, I haven't given it much thought."

"OK," said Big Owl. "Let's look at it this way. What did you do yesterday?"

With a bit of backwards thinking, Benny managed to remember what he had been doing the previous day.

"I flew to the grassy bank in the clearing to catch some mice for tea—I remember now."

"That's right," said Big Owl. "Now, *how* did you do that?"

"What do you mean *how*?"

"Take me through what was going through your mind just before you set off."

"Well, I … er … I did go through my pre-flight checklist, honest," he said quickly, hoping his dad wouldn't find out that he actually always skipped the bit about checking for lice on his wing tips.

"Let me take you through it slowly," interrupted Big Owl with a great deal of patience and just a hint of hurry-up-son-I-am-trying-toinvolve-you-in-a-Socratic-dialogue-here-but-please-get-a-move-on-as-I've-got-an-impor-tant-father-to-son-lesson-welling-up-inside-of-me-and-it-really-is-bursting-to-get-out.

"Before you set off, did you know where you were going?"

"Well, yes, the bank in the clearing."

"That's right. To the clearing bank. And what were you going there for?"

"Mice," said Benny. "'Lovely crunchy, fresh and jumpy, mice, mice, mice'," he continued, almost drooling as he recited the latest advertising jingle for Mousestretcher—for all your small rodent needs.

"And when did you have to get there by?"

"Well, I had to get there for three thirty," said Benny, before adding, "because that's when the bank shuts, although why they can't be open when I actually need them I don't kn—"

Big Owl interrupted his son. He too hated the banks but knew they were a necessary evil, like flatulence and newspapers. "So, you knew *where* you were going, *what* you were going for, *when* you wanted to get there and, I presume, *how* you were going to get there?"

"That's right. I always fly north from my house and turn left at the big beech tree."

"And why do you always go that way?"

"Because the poplar route is always too busy, that's why. And, anyway, I like going to the beech."

"And what if, one day, you found your normal route blocked? Then what would you do?"

"Well, I suppose I would just go a different way."

"And what if, when you got there, the bank was closed. Or they were all out of mice? What would you do then?"

"I would go somewhere else, I suppose. There's a Voles R Us just on the corner near Marble Larch."

"Exactly," said Big Owl with a sudden burst of joy. "Exactly, exactly, exactly," he continued, obviously very pleased with himself and doing a little dance with joy on the home branch. Then he stopped dancing, Joy excused herself and Big Owl said seriously, "So, you *know* exactly what to do."

And with that, happy that his task was going well, Big Owl closed one eye at a time and dropped off to sleep (which, when you are a bird thirty feet up a large tree, needs even more metaphorical emphasis than it does for humans, especially after that incident with Larry the Literal Owl, who always took everything at face value and spent a great deal of time in the Animal Hospital).

"I know what to do," said Benny to himself, part in puzzlement, part in wonder. "Yes, I suppose I do."

Oak: The Third
(only it isn't an oak)

The following day, with the sun sinking low in the sky and the owl day just beginning, Big Owl started the third lesson.

"Look around you," said Big Owl. "Look at the forest around you. What do you see?"

Benny, who was beginning to get the hang of actually looking and noticing now, started to look around him.

"Trees," he said triumphantly, then added, "wood" just so his dad didn't quote the obvious, "lots of it."

"And what sorts of trees, what type of wood, do you see, son?" continued Big Owl.

"Well, mostly oaks," said Benny.

"What about that tree over there, just beyond the dew pond and to the left of badger's stump."

Benny followed Big Owl's eyes but when he found they weren't going anywhere he looked instead towards the pond and the three-legged badger his dad had mentioned.

He saw a deep green tree, dark but powerful and, well, different from the others.

"Cedar tree," said Big Owl knowingly.

"Yes, I do see the tree," said Benny. "It's, well, different from the others, isn't it?"

"Yes, it is different. It doesn't look like the other trees: it has different bark, different leaves, a different greenness. It doesn't even lose its leaves in the winter like all the oaks. Yet it is still an important part of the wood, isn't it?"

"And so the tree-to-owl metaphor is …?" enquired Benny, now that he was getting the hang of the way his dad was working.

"Does that tree do what the other trees do?" asked Big Owl.

"Well, no, not really," replied Benny. "Sort of, but no."

"Yet it's still a successful tree even though others may look at it and resent the fact that it doesn't do what all the other trees do."

"Yes, I guess," said Benny.

"Now take a look at yourself. What are you like?"

"Me? I am, well, I'm like me," replied Benny still confused.

"Go on," encouraged Big Owl.

"Well, I do like the other owlets do, I wear what the other owlets wear, I hoot like the other owlets hoot—but then, hey, birds of a feather and all that," added Benny quickly, beginning to appreciate what Big Owl was getting at now.

"Yes, and you know what they say, if you want to fly with the eagles, don't scratch with the turkeys," added Big Owl just as quickly.

"So," began Benny falteringly, "what you're saying is ..."

"What I'm saying is you don't have to do what every other owl does. You don't have to do stuff just because all the other owls are doing it or because that's the way owls have always done it."

"So, you're telling me to ... be different," said Benny.

"Nope," replied Big Owl, "I'm telling you to be *creative*. Think independent. Fly your own flight. Do things no owl does or do things every owl does but in a way no owl does. And, son …" At this point Big Owl leaned forward slowly and meaningfully as if to whisper something of great secretive importance into the ear of his son. Benny leaned closer and tilted his ear towards his dad's beak. "Break the rules, son," whispered Big Owl, "break the rules."

Benny fluttered back in amazement. All his life he had been told to do what he was told, to do this, do that, clean your nest, don't speak with your beak full, a bird in the hand needs help, hoot before you leap. And now here was his dad telling him to go out and break the rules.

"Break the …" stuttered Benny.

Big Owl finished his son's sentence for him, "… the rules son, break the rules."

"So, Dad …" said Benny, his head reeling.

"Yes, son," said Big Owl, pleased with himself for having made such an impact on his son.

"Dad, you can't dance, you're embarrassing in front of my friends and I know what you and

Mum are up to when you hop into the tree trunk and close the bark."

"Son," replied Big Owl, "*not* the 'respect your parents at all times' rule."

"Oh," said Benny in an embarrassed way, going red—easy for a squirrel but more of a challenge for an owl. "Well, what do you mean, then?"

"I mean …" continued Big Owl making a mental note to wait until broad daylight next time he wanted to play "humans and bees" with Mrs Owl. "I mean you don't have to do what everyone says, not all the time. You don't have to ask permission, not all the time. Forgiveness every now and again all right, but not permission. So, make your mark, son. Remember you can until you can't. And then sometimes you still can. Do things your way. I'll say it again son." With this Big Owl lowered his voice to little more than a whisper, which, interestingly enough, had the same effect as if he had been shouting. "Fly your own flight," he said.

Benny started to feel a giddy sensation welling up from his gizzard and it made him dizzy. And a giddy owl with a dizzy gizzard is quite a special thing to behold. He gently unfolded his wings as he took his soft wing tips out of his pockets and slowly, so slowly, tensed himself, ready to soar off into the forest.

"Where are you going?" asked Big Owl in a worried way. "We're only three parts of the way through our thinking lessons."

"I just need to be alone for a while," said Benny, almost to himself, as he slid from the branch of the tree and beamed out on his broad silent wings. "I'll see you soon," he added, sliding gracefully into the singing green veil. "I just want to fly my own flight for a while."

Oak: The Fourth

Benny flew silently around the forest for several hours, lost in his own thoughts.

He was beginning to realise how much freedom he really had. The freedom to do anything he needed to do. To be whatever he needed to be. And that freedom, the thought of a life with the walls gone, was a scary thought to be thinking. It was like learning to fly all over again. He remembered what his mother had said to him when he had been getting ready to fly for the very first time. "You've got to leave the nest if you want to fly, son." And she was right, too.

But what he realised now was that there was another nest to leave, but this one wasn't a real one made of twigs and moss and lollipop sticks with bad jokes on them: it was in his head.

As he flew round and round, he wasn't quite sure whether to be frightened or excited by the things his father had been telling him. He decided, after some deliberation, that he was both excited *and* frightened by it all, something that made his heart quicken and his eyes grow wide, which, when you're an owl, is not that easy to spot.

"At least," he said to himself, "with all this scary newfound freedom to do anything I want to, I have my dad to help me decide *what* to do. And especially what *not* to do. At least he's around to look out for me."

These thoughts reassured him a little as he made up his mind to fly back to his tree to continue his thinking lessons with his dad.

"Hurts, doesn't it?" said Big Owl when he saw Benny alighting on the branch next to him.

"You bet, Dad," replied Benny. "All this thinking, all these discoveries, all these changes. It *does* hurt."

"No," replied Big Owl. "I just stubbed my claw on one of those knobbly bits on the branch. What are you talking about?"

"No ... well ... it was just ..." stuttered Benny. "Never mind. What's next, Dad? Have I learned all I need to know?"

Big Owl looked sternly at Benny. "Are you dead?" he asked curtly.

"No, I was just sleeping," said Curtly.

"No, not you, I was talking to my son."

"Oh, sorry," said Curtly.

"Well, Benny?"

"Er, no ..." replied Benny. "Of course I'm not dead."

"Then you still have things to learn," continued Big Owl. "Now look at this tree that we are standing on. The Home Tree. What makes it so strong?"

"Well, it's made of wood for a start," replied Benny, combining haste with optimism in equal measure.

"And that's it, is it?" replied Big Owl disparagingly—easy for an owl, tricky for a sparrow.

"Erm, probably not. Cut to the chase, Dad. My brain hurts," said Benny.

"This grand old oak tree is surrounded by other oaks, isn't it? But do they hold it up? Do they support it physically? Do their branches carry the load of our Home Tree?"

"Well, no."

"No, that's right. But they *do* help it grow straight and true, don't they?"

"True," said Benny.

"And straight," said Big Owl.

"Straight up?" said Benny.

"Cross my heart," replied Big Owl. "The other trees help, are there, uphold and protect, but at the end of the night our Home Tree supports itself."

Benny nodded thoughtfully and then had a go thinking noddingly until he reverted to the first action. He thought about the times he had spent on the Home Tree. It was the first home he had ever known. From the moment he opened his egg it was there: its wonderful easy branches that sailed with the wind, its shimmering summer coat, the great trunk, so strong and sturdy, filled with sap. He remembered that, as a very young owl, he had loved the taste of the trunk and was always asking his mother if he could lick the bole.

He thought of the tree's great haunches, where it eased itself up from the soil, and in his mind's eye he pictured, stretching in a huge caring web beneath the tree, the roots, sucking goodness from the soil and squirting it up to the branches and leaves above it. Benny had always especially liked the idea that you could take a tree in winter and turn it upside down and no one would notice.

"And the owly slant?" enquired Benny, although he had a rough idea of what was coming next.

"The owly slant," replied Big Owl, narrowing his eyes, "is that *you* need to think like the oak. I'm here for you, son, but I am not doing it for you. I can support you but I can't always hold you up. You know those trees that have been captured and tamed by the humans? The ones that they grow in their gardens tied to stakes and posts? They may grow big but do they grow strong? And what happens when wind and circumstance blow them loose from their support? Hopeless alone is the windblown tree who has never stood alone."

Benny knew Big Owl had a point. He didn't like the point, but could feel himself being prodded with it all the same.

Big Owl continued, "I want you to do well. But I can't want it for you more than you want it for yourself. *You* are responsible for your own success, Benny. No one else."

This, Benny realised, was his fourth lesson. The lesson of responsibility.

"Take this one lesson on board and you will see immediate changes," continued Big Owl. "Be strong enough to stand yourself up and, no matter what happens, you will always win."

Benny thought for a while about the idea of responsibility, about the strong oak, about the roots. Then the Great Wind came into his head.

"Beg pardon!" said Big Owl. "It's the spicy food I had last night." He had had a lichen curry the previous night as well as a vole korma—easy for an owl, trickier for a cormorant.

Benny ignored his dad's windy troubles, as you are supposed when it's your parents. There was still one thing troubling him about what his dad was saying.

"Dad, if oaks are so strong …" he began.

"Yes?" said Big Owl, intrigued to know what was coming next.

"Then how come in the Big Wind last year at least three of them went roots up?"

"Ah, well," replied Big Owl with calm assurance, "that's the problem with oaks: they're so inflexible."

Oak: The Fifth

The following day Benny woke up at the crack of dusk and wondered what lay ahead. He knew what laid an egg but laying a head was a totally different matter.

He was thinking about times when he had faced up to things he had feared in the past. Like the first time he had flown beyond the forest and out across the open farmland. It wasn't so bad, was it? But you had to do it in order to know that. There are some things you can't go round. You have to go through. That seemed to be the only way to get rid of the scary feelings he had about the landscape beyond the forest. "Fear the field and do it anyway" as the saying goes—sort of.

He felt a growing sense of waking up, of growing up, of having so much before him, so many things to do, so much to explore, so many adventures to have. All he needed to do was to work out where he wanted to go and ... basically ... sort of ... well ... just set off in that direction.

Then his careering thoughts were interrupted by the sight of his dad, toddling along the branch with his feathers a flutter as he flapped off the day's sleep.

"Oak Number Five?" he asked his son with a smile on his face (which was where he kept it: it was the best place he'd found and he had tried several other places before he had found that one).

"Oak Number Five," said Benny earnestly. "Let's do it."

Big Owl looked around him intently, something he had learned from the scouts who came camping in the forest in the summer. Then he stopped looking and took a deep pleased-with-himself breath. The fifth oak would be the one they were on. Sometimes you can be so busy looking around you, you miss where you are.

"Where are you?" asked Big Owl.

"I'm here," replied Benny, waving, thinking that perhaps one of Big Owl's three eyelids wasn't working properly and he couldn't see him. "Where *exactly*?" continued Big Owl, whose one-for-blinking, one-for-sleeping and one-for-cleaning eyelids were working fine. Although winking always took him a while.

"On the Home Tree, in the forest, in the centre of the world," replied Benny with precision.

"And are you alone?" asked Big Owl in a mat-ter-of-fact sort of way, which, as a matter of fact, was quite off-putting for Benny.

"Well, no," he replied. "You're here, aren't you?"

Big Owl looked frustrated for a brief moment and then, regaining his composure, continued with all the patience only a father could muster.

"Are *we* alone, then?"

Benny looked around him, which for an owl involves standing very still and swivelling your head around in a way that really frightened the other birds, especially if you did it when they least expected it. He had met a swallow one summer that had tried it but had got stuck halfway round and had died after flying north for the winter.

"I think ... we are alone," replied Benny hesitantly.

"OK," continued Big Owl. "If that's the case, what's that by your foot?"

"My other foot," replied Benny.

"No, the other side," snapped Big Owl, easy for a crocodile, harder for an owl with an overhanging top beak.

Benny looked down and noticed a small green caterpillar caterpulling itself along the branch in search of leaves and things.

"Where did he come from?" said Benny feigning surprise.

"And what about that?" continued Big Owl, nodding his head towards a large spider's web that trembled like a lace curtain pulled across one of the oak's many crannies.

"Who put that there?" said Benny, again trying to cover up what he now realised he had missed before.

"You're beginning to open your eyes. Now clear the feathers from your top and bottom ears. What's that awful racket you can hear splitting branches from the top of the trees? I don't suppose you have noticed the Song Thrush up there, have you?"

Benny Owl looked sheepish, something that involved lying on his back with his feet in the air pretending he couldn't get up.

"Get up," said Big Owl.

"OK," said Benny quietly, getting up.

"Now," continued Big Owl. "This oak is full of life—spiders, insects, fungus, birds, squirrels. The Home Tree is home to more than just us owls, isn't it?"

"Yes, I guess," said Benny.

"We are, though, very different in how we go about life on the tree, aren't we? Yet we have all learned to live in the same oak."

"Yes," said Benny hesitantly knowing that his fifth lesson was on its way, as steady and inexorable as a big red steady inexorable thing but not as red. "So, lesson number five is …?"

"Lesson number five, my dear son, is the learning lesson. To know that we are different, but that we can all learn and learn well. So, you have to learn how *you* learn best—know how you learn, learn the way your brain needs to learn and learn in many different ways."

Benny looked blank for while, trying to take on board what his father was saying.

"Nope," he said finally, "you've lost me there again. Take me through that one more time."

"OK," replied Big Owl. "Let's see if you can get to grips with it this way."

Benny started to feel better straightaway.

"Some learn best by *seeing* the learning—think of the hawk with his keen, keen eyes. What he sees, he catches. Some learn best by *hearing* the learning. Think about the bats whose language is so high you have to stand on tiptoe to hear it.

"And …" interrupted Benny, who thought he knew what was coming next. "And some learn best by having it up their nose, don't they? Like that time when I called Tyrone Owl a 'scrawny' owl, and I made that joke that he was the owl who put the 'owl' in 'sick bowl' and then he pinned me down and stuck earwigs up my nose. He said *that* was to teach me a lesson."

"Well, sort of," continued Big Owl, "but that wasn't quite what I had in mind. What I was *going* to say was that some learn best by *doing* the learning, like the young squirrels we see learning to leap between the branches—"

"And the ones we see learning to plummet vertically and squeal at the same time," interrupted Benny excitedly.

"Yes, the clumsy ones learn very quickly," said Big Owl sadly, "too late, but very quickly. Now, when we learn, we will learn best if we do a bit of it all."

"So," continued Benny, picking up the baton where his father had left it, "if when we learn we spend some time doing like the hawk, some time doing like the bat and some time doing like squirrels …"

"*Some* of the squirrels."

"*Some* of the squirrels. If we do a bit of all these then we, we …"

"Then we learn best," said Big Owl taking back the baton, shaking off the bat and finishing Benny's sentence for him. "But that's not all. We also need to remember that we all—each and every one of us in the forest—have our own special areas of genius that allow us to be clever in our own ways. Let me elaborate."

And here Big Owl took a deep breath, and then began.

"The spider knows how to create a perfect web with just the right geometry in just the right place to catch the flies—it's logical to her.

"The butterfly flashes her wings to betray the most outstanding colours and patterns—she's a visual genius.

"The thrush can sing to thrushes all round the forest with her awful screeching—but it's musical delight to some.

"The ant is a physical genius, so strong but as small as, as …"

"As an ant?" suggested Benny helpfully.

"Yes, that's right. As small as an ant but such a physical giant.

"The squirrel actually helps keep the forest going, planting acorns and beech nuts in the autumn, that they will come to seed in the spring to regenerate the forest—he is the great gardener."

"But not much of a flyer, though, eh, Dad?" laughed Benny making a whoosh-splat sort of motion with one of his wings.

"Well, actually, son," said Big Owl crossly, "you may mock but I have heard it said in a forest a long, long way from this one there is a squirrel that can fly thanks to a special sort of T-shirt it wears."

Benny looked closely at his father's face to see whether he was being serious or pulling his primaries, like the time he had told him about the singing cows that lived under the water or how some of the forest creatures hatched from eggs in a nest inside their mummy's tummy.

"The bee—apart from being a great dancer—is also a very sociable little soul in her furry vest and bonnet. She works so well as part of the team.

"Yet the Robin, with his red breast, can't stand the sight of his fellow birds, living a solitary life of quiet reflection and eating worms.

"The woodpecker is a great communicator. You can hear him all round the forest tap-tap-tapping his messages to his fellow woodpeckers. Tap-tap-tapping his love calls. Tap-tap-tapping the fact that he is alive and glad of it. Tap-tap-tapping the fact that he has a beak and is not afraid to use it. Tap, tap, tap, tap, tap, tap, *tap, tap, TAP*! Damn you, you pointy-beaked, feather-brained power drills, stop that infernal tap-tap-tapping!"

"Steady, Dad," said Benny. "Get a grip."

"Sorry," said Big Owl, pulling himself together. "It's just that constant tap-tap-tapping."

"Yes, Dad, it's OK. I get the point. And anyway, they're not all like that, are they? My mate

Roger is quite a nice woodpecker, even if he is a bit wet."

"Exactly!" exclaimed Big Owl. "And there's nothing more annoying than a tapping drip."

"Now, Dad, let's get back to the lesson. You were telling me about the different strengths of the creatures of the forest."

"Oh, yes," said Big Owl, "where was I?"

"Woodpeckers," suggested Benny.

"Oh, yes, the great communicators. Well, now, there you are. Eight different areas of genius. Don't ask how clever you are, son: ask instead *how* are you clever? Where does your intelligence lie? Because once you know that, once you understand the genius within, then you will start to learn how to learn and succeed by playing to your own strengths."

"But," said Benny who was clearly troubled by something, "if I learned by playing to my strengths and using the whole range of different intelligences in a variety of different ways, surely that would not only mean I would learn more *and* learn more quickly, but it would also make learning fun and enjoyable."

Big Owl thought for a while. "Yes, you're exactly right, son. But don't tell anyone or they'll all be doing it, and, if everyone started learning well, then where would we be? You have to keep it to yourself, son, for the sake of forest order. After all, we don't want the lower creatures getting above themselves, do we?"

Oak: The Sixth

"Dad, I've got a problem," said Benny when he perched next to Big Owl the following night.

"There's no such thing as a problem, just an opportunity," replied Big Owl with relish.

"What are you on about?" replied Benny, without relish but with a side order of fries. "If that's the case, then Wayne Badger, the young hooligan who was caught beating up old ladybirds and playing with fireflies, would be an 'opportunity child'."

"Well, I suppose he is," replied Big Owl thoughtfully, pleased by his son's logic. But, then again, that is what sometimes happens when you take things to their logical conclusion—it makes them all nonsensical and then they often come out better.

"OK, son," continued Big Owl, "what's your 'problem'?" And then, just before Benny could speak, he raised one wing to stop him and then added, "No, I'll change that. I don't want to help you solve your problem."

"Oh, thanks a lot," said Benny, hurt.

"No, I will do something more useful. I will help you to solve *problems*."

"Ah," said Benny, "this will be Number Six, then, will it?"

"I think we can say so," said Big Owl.

"Which oak are we going to work with today?" asked Benny looking around him for a tree that could be used somehow or other for problem solving.

"All of them," replied Big Owl knowingly.

"All of them?" asked Benny in a surprised tone.

"All of them," reaffirmed Big Owl, adding, "to begin with."

Benny decided it was time to get himself comfortable, took a deep breath and readied himself for his next lesson.

"Pick a tree," said Big Owl after a few minutes' thought, "any tree."

"OK," said Benny, looking around him with one of those 360-degree owl-head things, "got one."

Owl looked expectantly at Benny, who, in turn, was looking expectantly back again.

"Well?" said Big Owl.

"Oh, you want me to tell you which one?" asked Benny.

"Yes!" snapped Big Owl—easy for a branch but not so easy for an owl standing on one.

"Oh, sorry," replied Benny. "I thought it was one of your magic tricks. Like the time you pulled the rabbit out of that burrow," continued Benny, "and then you ate it."

"No, no," said Big Owl impatiently.

"Or when mum used to pull mice out of her beak," continued Benny warming to the magic theme, "and then *I* ate it," he added with a look of distaste.

"Look, son," said Big Owl crossly, "there's a world of difference between prestidigitation and regurgitation. Now, shut your beak and tell me which tree you want to start with."

"OK," said Benny smally, "how about that one over there, with the crows nesting in it?" And he pointed with one of his wing tips.

"Right," continued Big Owl, getting back into his stride. "Let's see if you're getting the hang of this. If that tree were to represent an approach to solving problems, what might it be?"

Benny thought for a while and then said, "I don't know."

"Well, what if you did know?" replied Big Owl quickly.

"Um … I suppose …"

"Yes, go on."

"I suppose the crows could represent the problems themselves—dark and scary, never standing still and keeping you awake, and constantly dropping poo on you from a great height and …"—Benny was definitely beginning to get the hang of it now—"and making so much noise you can't hear yourself hoot and all frightening with their big starey eyes and those baggy trousers and every time you think you've got rid of one another pops up from somewhere …."

"Very good, son," said Big Owl proudly. "And the tree itself, what about the tree?"

"The tree? Why, that represents the fact that beneath every problem you will find a bigger cause holding it up—being the trunk—and beneath that an even deeper cause or root—being the root." Benny was very pleased with his newfound creativity. "That's it, isn't it? That's the answer. I'm right, aren't I, Dad?"

"Yes, you are, son," replied Big Owl. "Now choose another tree."

"Another one?" said Benny, surprised.

"Another one."

"Why, what was wrong with the first answer?"

"Just choose one and you will see. You don't know until you do."

"OK, well, what about that one over there, where the trunk is split in two? What about that one?"

"You tell me. How could that one represent an approach to problem solving?"

"Well," Benny pondered—easy for an owl but not for a panda, "I suppose ..."

"Yes?" encouraged Big Owl. "What do you suppose?"

"I suppose you could say that quite often what looks like one big problem is sometimes more than one problem, so ..." Benny paused while he tracked down the deeper message that he knew was there. (That in itself made Benny pause still further—which is the best sort of pause, a still one. How did he know the answer was there even though he didn't know the answer? He felt that this would probably constitute Oak: The Seventh. Though he didn't know.)

"So, when you have a problem, well ..."

"Yes ...?"

"When you have a problem you break it down into its smaller parts and do them one at a time," said Benny, finishing with a breathless flourish.

"Very good," said Big Owl in a way that meant Benny knew he hadn't finished yet.

"Now choose another one," he said.

"Another one?" said Benny with horror.

"I'll tell you what," interrupted Big Owl, "let me choose."

"OK," said Benny warily.

"That one," said Big Owl with a triumphant

gesture of his wing tips that ended in the best pointy sort of gesture an owl with rounded wing tips can manage. Few members of the woodland community appreciate how hard it is for an owl to point, a problem by its very nature impossible for an owl to point out, which is why they get the hawks to do it for them.

Benny followed the general direction of Big Owl's soft white feathers, and, after a while, noticed the rotting carcass of an immense old oak lying partly submerged under brambles and that stringy sort of weed with the big trumpets. He thought it might be part of the brassica section but he wasn't sure.

"That dead one?" asked Benny, hoping he had it wrong.

"Dead, is it?" replied Big Owl mysteriously. "Hmmmm!"

Benny thought to himself. The oak tree had been hit by lightning in the Great Storm many years ago. Since that time it had lain there slowly rotting, sinking into a rising swamp of brambles and weeds and becoming home to legions of beetles, spiders, woodlice and those little squidgy insects with sulky faces. But no small sheep.

"I know," said Benny suddenly. "The dead oak stands for the fact that nothing lasts for ever and, no matter how mighty a problem looks now, one day it will be conquered."

He looked in triumph at his dad, who blinked slowly, one eye at a time, and said simply, "What else?"

"What else?" said Benny, crestfallen—easy for a jay but harder for an owl.

"What else?" replied Big Owl quietly.

"Erm …" Benny started the thinking process all over again, repeating to himself, "What else? What else?"

"I know," he flashed again. "When you have a big problem sometimes it doesn't look so big when you come at it a different way, when you look from a different angle. The oak doesn't look so huge once it's on the ground and, as they say, a tree is best measured when it's down. That's it, isn't it? It must be." Benny looked expectantly at Big Owl again.

Big Owl, however, simply returned the expectant look, much to Benny's annoyance—something that made the look more expectorant than expectant—and said again, "What else?"

"What *else*?" spluttered Benny. "I don't know, I give up. I give you some brilliant answers and you say they're wrong."

"No!" insisted Big Owl, raising a wing to stop his son's anger in its tracks. "I never said they were wrong, did I?"

Benny reflected for a minute—easy for a pond but more of an art for an owl.

"Well, if they're not wrong, which one is the *right* answer, then?"

"They *all* are," replied Big Owl. "Now, what else?"

"But … very … you … erm … it's just …" Benny was spluttering again, always a good sign that his reality was getting bigger.

"What else?" pressed Big Owl.

"OK," said Benny, hopping from foot to foot. "OK, OK. And … the … what about …? I know, what about, no matter how big the problem, there is always something positive to come out of it. That oak came crashing to earth but in doing so it is providing a home for all sorts of plants and insects and animals. But no small sheep."

Big Owl smiled.

"And …" said Benny quickly before his dad had a chance to interrupt. "And, also, sometimes a huge problem can be laid low by a flash of inspiration, like the lightning that brought down the tree. And sometimes your problems get solved when you least expect them to, and in unexpected, unforeseen ways. And sometimes what seems like a tiny little problem may actually be something quite huge. After all, no matter how big the oak, it is only ever three letters big. And … and … and …"

"I think," interrupted by the owl, "I think you are getting the big picture."

"Well, no, actually," responded Benny. "I've given you loads of answers. Which *one* is right?"

"Don't you see?" replied Big Owl. "They all are."

Benny's brain made that sort of "oomph" sound as it audibly expanded.

Big Owl continued. "Nothing," he said, "nothing is more dangerous than an oak when it is the only oak you have. If you try to solve the problem with the *first* right answer that comes your way, then there is no guarantee that you'll be solving it with the *best* right answer. You have to come up with as many right answers as you can and then—and this is the gilded rule of problem solving—evaluate second. You should fly narrow only once you've flown broad."

"So ..." said Benny, trying—and not for the first time—to get his little feathery head around what his dad was telling him. "So, all of those answers were right but some were *more* right than others?"

"Precisely," replied Big Owl with a smile.

"Ooh," said Benny in a very small sort of way. "Ooh!"

As they had been speaking, neither of them had noticed that the wind had started to pick up and the forest was hissing with the sound of a million shaking leaves.

As the approaching storm entered the consciousness of the two owls they both raised their eyes to the treacling sky and dug deeper with their claws into the Home Branch.

"Any more lessons?" asked Benny, looking expectantly at his father.

"Seven is a good number," replied Big Owl enigmatically.

"One to go, then?" said Benny.

"One to go," replied Big Owl.

Oak: The Seventh

The storm was fantastic to be part of. It started with a blackening of the high sky that put every single quivering leaf of every tree into pinpoint definition as they were lit by golden, bursting light squeezing from under the storm clouds.

The light. Then the wind. Wind that bristled and whipped up excitement from root to tip of the forest, each leaf a rustling quiver as the storm rolled unstoppably onto the wood.

Then the dry chatter of the leaves was slowly replaced by a greater hiss, not excited like the trees, but gassy and ominous.

And then it was here, moving through the trees like a beautiful woman in a crowded room, intoxicating the forest with its smell, its sight, its basic, glorious nature.

Benny, meanwhile, was missing all this as he had hopped into the trunk to pick mites out of his plumage with his beak.

While he was preening he was also thinking to himself. (With all the things he now felt he knew, thinking to other people seemed to be harder than ever.)

In particular there were three things bothering him. The first was how he had known that there would be a seventh oak and that it would be the last for now. The second was that, when he and his father had realised that the storm was coming, neither of them was surprised. It was as if they had known it was coming before they had realised it was on its way.

"There must be an answer to the two puzzles, I know it," said Benny quietly to himself. And this was the third source of confusion. How did he *know* that there must be an answer?

Outside, the storm had finished its stride through the forest and Benny decided to hop back out to see if his dad was around to finish off the lesson and sort out that nagging feeling that he was noticing, not so much in his head as in his gut.

The sun was having a quick look round to make sure it was safe to come back out, and from every beaded twig and leaf its reflected light hung and trembled in the peace of the newly cleaned forest.

From nowhere, Big Owl landed beside his son on the Home Branch, sending a pocket full of diamonds cascading onto the forest floor below, narrowly missing a bee that was just coming out of hiding from underneath a large toadstool but scoring a direct hit on a toad that was trying unsuccessfully to hide underneath a beestool.

"Good storm, eh, Dad, as storms go?" said Benny happily.

"Oh, yes," replied Big Owl, "they always go."

"Dad?" continued Benny. "Have you ever had that feeling when you know but you don't know, like, all at the same time?"

"I know I don't know what you mean," said Big Owl teasingly.

"Oh, Dad," said Benny, exasperated. "Put that teasel down and listen. It's important. I'm not a kid any more." Easy for an owlet to say but not for a goatlet.

Dad put his serious face on and said, "OK, tell me what you mean."

"Well," started Benny, "sometimes I know I know the answer ..."

"You know you know," murmured Big Owl, showing he was listening.

"But", continued Benny, "I also know that I know I don't know."

"You know you don't know," continued Big Owl in a similar vein.

"Do you know what I mean?" asked Benny in desperation.

"No!" said Big Owl.

"Oh," said Benny.

"Or, rather," continued Big Owl, "I do and I don't."

"Exactly!" replied Benny excitedly. "You know and you don't know. That's exactly it!" And he looked expectantly at his father.

Big Owl looked up to the sky to help him capture the picture of his son when he was much younger, just a chick, a bubble of fluff with a constantly gaping beak.

"When you were young, just after you had stuck your little egg tooth out of the egg, do you remember that?"

Benny thought for while and realised he couldn't remember that far back.

"Well, no, basically," he said, afraid of disappointing his father. He need not have worried.

"Exactly!" continued Big Owl. "Even when you were first coming into this world and you can't even remember anything about it, you still knew what to do, didn't you?"

"What do you mean, 'knew what to do'?" asked Benny, confused, and not for the first time. Or the last, he felt.

"Who told you *how* to come out of your shell? Or when?"

"Well, no one, I suppose," pondered Benny.

"Exactly, no one ever does. And who told you how to get your mother to give you food? And who told you how to stay quiet when you heard loud noises outside? And who taught you how to fly?"

"Well," stumbled Benny. "I just sort of did it all, didn't I?"

"Exactly," said Big Owl again. "You knew what to do. You *know* what to do."

"But *how* did I know what do?" asked Benny in a pleading sort of voice. "Who *taught* me?"

"You did," replied Big Owl with conviction. "From deep down inside, you knew."

"I knew?" asked Benny in a small voice.

"You always know," replied Big Owl in a dramatic tone.

"You mean …?" continued Benny, the message that his dad was trying to share with him slowly beginning to drop.

"Yes," said Big Owl firmly. "Gizzard wisdom."

"Wow!" said Benny in a whisper.

"Intuition," said Big Owl knowingly. "There's a clue in the word, don't you think?"

Benny did think. "What? 'iti'?" he asked.

"No," tutted Big Owl, "the first two letters."

"Oh," said Benny suddenly getting it.

"Exactly," said Big Owl who had had it all the time.

"In," continued Benny, who once he'd got it wasn't going to let it go.

"In …" continued Big Owl, "… tuition."

"So, what you're saying is, that there are times when I just know. When I have the answer, from deep down inside."

Yes," said Big Owl with authority. "It knows, you know."

"But …" interrupted Benny suddenly, obviously troubled. "The dead oak, the oak with all the different sorts of intelligence, the problem-solving oaks—all of them."

"Yes?" continued Big Owl.

"Well, where is the oak that stands for this 'trust the gut, intuition, gizzard wisdom' way of thinking?"

Big Owl thought for a while, then looked

around himself. Then he looked around Benny. Then he just looked around.

"What are you looking for, Dad?" asked Benny in an excited tone.

"I don't know," replied Big Owl. "But I will when I find it."

The sun was coming up outside the wood's edge, groping its way between the trees with its brilliant outstretched arms, prodding awake the birds and animals of the forest. Even the flowers unclenched themselves from the thick darkness of the night. The wood was blinking itself awake, except for the owl, solitary hunters in the lonely night. Solitary, except for the foxes who kept the owls company in their nocturnal lifestyle. Just the owls and the foxes in a dark, silent wood. Just the owls and the foxes—and the badgers, colleagues of the night. The three races silently roaming the thickened light of the night-time woods. Oh, and the bats, screaming silently to themselves as they plucked moths so deftly from the night air that all that was left was two discarded and vaguely confused wings, fluttering to the forest floor.

But apart from the owls, the foxes, the badgers, the bats, the moths and even the little voles and shrews that make it worthwhile for the owls to come out anyway—apart from all that, night-time was a serene and quiet place in the woods. And dawn brought a coming-to-life sort of movement that Big Owl was studying closely while Benny studied Big Owl equally closely.

"There!" exclaimed Big Owl, suddenly causing Benny to jump equally suddenly.

"Where?" asked Benny.

"Up there, in the treetops."

Benny followed his dad's gaze and there, up in the highest branches of the trees, he could just make out the shape of a squirrel, clambering deftly about, its fur-thick tail silhouetted by the high, pale dawn sky.

"That's the oak I'm looking for," said Big Owl.

Benny looked puzzled for a while. Then he tried looking confused but decided that puzzled was easier to cope with.

"What ...?" Benny began hesitantly. "You mean the oak the squirrel is in?"

"No," replied Big Owl, obviously pleased with himself. "I mean the squirrel the oak is in."

Lastly

Edgar Owl was flapping about on the Home Branch, practising the stretch and flex movement so useful for owls flying into small holes such as tree trunks, church windows and postboxes. (This last manoeuvre also involved a breathe-in-and-squeeze sort of movement that was quite difficult to achieve for an owl and generally avoided. But it was in the book all the same.)

"Dad," said Edgar when he saw his father alight on the home branch next to him. "You're on fire again, Dad."

"Whoops! Sorry about that," said Benny, flapping his wings to put out the flames.

"Anyway, Dad, how come you're so old and wise?" asked Edgar earnestly.

"Well," said Benny with a knowing owl smile. "The 'old' bit just sort of happens. As for the wise bit, well, where shall we begin?" And he looked around himself at the beauty of the oak-thick forest.